From Disgrace to Grace

Honoring the Word of God

MARY ROBINSON

iUniverse, Inc.
Bloomington

FROM DISGRACE TO GRACE
HONORING THE WORD OF GOD

iUniverse books may be ordered through booksellers or by contacting:

iUniverse
1663 Liberty Drive
Bloomington, IN 47403
www.iuniverse.com
1-800-Authors (1-800-288-4677)

Because of the dynamic nature of the Internet, any web addresses or links contained in this book may have changed since publication and may no longer be valid. The views expressed in this work are solely those of the author and do not necessarily reflect the views of the publisher, and the publisher hereby disclaims any responsibility for them.

Any people depicted in stock imagery provided by Thinkstock are models, and such images are being used for illustrative purposes only.

Certain stock imagery © Thinkstock.

ISBN: 978-1-4759-7159-0 (hc)
ISBN: 978-1-4759-7160-6 (sc)
ISBN: 978-1-4759-7158-3 (e)

Library of Congress Control Number: 2013900780

Printed in the United States of America

iUniverse rev. date: 1/28/2013

DEDICATION

I dedicate *From Disgrace to Grace* to all men and women. I hope to help educate those who read this book on studying the word of God and to send a message conveying how much God loves us. He wants us to live happy and blessed lives. However, we must honor his laws to receive his promises. God wants no one to perish; that's why he sent his son, Jesus Christ, to save us from the sins of this world. His only desire on judgment day is to have the pleasure of bringing all his children into eternal life! Let this be a reminder to change your mind-set to do God's will, honor his word, and eliminate the sin in your life. This defeats Satan at his own game and sends him into hell's eternal fire!

CONTENTS

ACKNOWLEDGMENTS

My inspiration for writing this book comes from my own personal experiences. I hope to send a message to help free others from the bondage and struggles they may be facing in their lives.

First and foremost, I would like to give thanks to my Lord and Savior for the insight and knowledge he gave me to write this book advising his people to study the word of God. Those who study the Bible will be inspired to change their mind-sets and habits to be delivered out of darkness by the grace he's given us through his son, Jesus Christ!

I would like to acknowledge some of the pastors who gave me wisdom and inspiration on my spiritual journey. Pastor Donald Battle baptized me when I was born again. He ministered to me about changing my mind-set by honoring the word of God and living a life that is pleasing to God. He told me that God loves me no matter what I've done in my life. I will always remember this pastor and his wife, Gwen Battle, from Divine Faith Ministries in Jonesboro, Georgia. They are great spiritual leaders.

I also want to thank Dr. Creflo Dollar, from World Changers Ministries in Atlanta, Georgia. He is one of my favorites. I have learned so much from his television ministry. He guarantees God can deliver you from any troubles in your life. He's a great teacher of the word of God. Pastor Joyce Meyers is a great woman of God. She doesn't cut corners; her teaching gets right to the point. The powerful and explosive Bishop T. D. Jakes is a much-anointed man of God. I got the title for my book through his television ministry; he taught a series on moving from disgrace to grace. Thank you, Bishop T. D. Jakes, for your intellect and wisdom.

After I moved back to Florida from Atlanta, Georgia, I joined the Faith Center in Sunrise, Florida, led by Bishop Henry Fernandez. I have been a member of his church for only a short time, but I have found Bishop Fernandez to be a man of great integrity and honor. He delivers God's word in a manner that motivates believers to understand God's plans. I am proud to be a member of his church.

These pastors all played a very important part in my spiritual life. I give God all the honor and praise for their wisdom and knowledge, which helped me write this book.

INTRODUCTION

From Disgrace to Grace exposes the realities of this world and shows how we as people have forgotten the morals and values by which we should live. We have taken God's grace and turned it into disgrace by neglecting to honor the word of God, failing to see how his laws apply to our lives.

We have to start acknowledging the wisdom that God has supplied humankind with to discern right from wrong. We can change our mind-sets to honor the word of God and live righteously by obeying his laws. We need to humble ourselves to live godly lives; our choices affect how our future unfolds. We parents must lead by example, teaching our children about the word of God, bringing them up in the right way, setting standards to respect the moral values that keep our families strong.

We must apply wisdom to prevent Satan's deception from destroying us with sins such as adultery and fornication. These sins are two of the most ultimate sins and cause great destruction to humankind and God's covenant with us. We must take back our proper place as humans by destroying Satan's disgrace and honoring God's grace, which saved us from being condemned!

CHAPTER 1
My Personal Testimony

I would like to share my personal testimony and expose the experiences I had with adultery and fornication. I believe these two sins are some of the most corruptive, and they are destroying the covenant between God and humankind. I say it this way because most people don't consider these sins to be harmful. I didn't view them that way either. I made excuses to overlook the wrong I was doing because the majority of people in my life were living this way too!

When you live in the world and do as the world does, you fail to recognize your sinful nature. If you recognize it, you tend to push it to the back of your mind, accepting this behavior as normal, just as the world does. *We have no peace of mind because we know what we are doing is wrong, but we continue to do it and fail to realize the truth!*

When I was younger, I had several relationships with single men and married men. As I grew older, I continued this behavior. I knew that I was doing wrong, and I still chose to do what others were doing.

I found out later in my life that this was not acceptable in the kingdom of God. He does not condone such behavior; he prescribes marriage. My last affair was with a married man. I was also married at that time and had been separated from my husband for some years. My husband and I had no children or property together. I was only married on paper; I was living as if I were a single woman.

I had an affair with this man for ten years. We did not live together, for he was still living at home with his family. We saw each other every week when time allowed. I had fallen in love with this man, and we became very fond of each other. I was getting ready to retire from my job and relocate to Georgia, and he was going to come with me. We started making plans to be with each other after he left his wife. However, when the time came, he told me he couldn't leave. He said he had to take care of some things first and would join me later. Well, later never came. At that point I got frustrated and dropped the relationship.

It was after I moved to Georgia that I became saved. In addition to the frustration I felt with the man, I ended the relationship out of a choice to sin no more. Now, this wasn't easy to do because I loved this man; it was painful to let go. I asked for God's help to get through it, and he helped me. He picked me up and put me on solid ground, and he pulled me out of the pit I was in, as the psalmist describes. He took my burdens and made them his. He sustained me when I felt the desire to be with a man. I felt so free and relieved, and my spirit was at rest.

When I was unpacking some books, I ran across a book titled *How to Find God*. I couldn't remember at the time how I got the book, but later I remembered that my roommate Deborah had given it to me as a gift. I started reading it, and the knowledge from that book made me realize how God wanted me to live my life. It led me to Christ, and I haven't looked back since.

I've learned that once you become saved, your spirit focuses on righteousness and helps you change your mind-set to live a godly life. I truly want to obey God and live right. I see now what Jesus meant when he said in Matthew 11:28 that he comes to give us rest; it's as if a load drops off of you. You know that you are in his protection, and he's right there with you.

When I was planning my move, everything went smoothly and fell right into place, as if someone else was directing my path. I had recently purchased a new car, rewarding myself on my retirement from the Postal Service. I planned to stay in the same place until my car was paid off. Unexpectedly, I paid it off in two years. I guess it was through the grace of God that I paid it off so quickly.

I think God directed my steps to take me out of my situation so that I would focus on him. My plan was to join a church when I moved to Georgia, and reading that book helped me make up my mind. If I had stayed in Florida, I would probably still be in that relationship, deceived by this world and believing that I was living right.

Unfortunately, Georgia was not what I expected. I stayed only one year before I moved back to Florida. However, I'm not the same person who left. I am now a born-again Christian, a child of the Most High God! As in my life, God will sometimes direct your steps to get you out of your present situation to one that helps you focus on him. It worked for me! I've been changed, freed, and delivered!

My ex learned of my return, but we no longer have a romantic relationship; we're just friends. I love him like my neighbor, with no animosity and seeking no revenge toward him. I wish and pray that he gets his life together and finds God like I did, and I will do anything I can to help him.

God gave me a revelation of who I am and whose I am. He showed me my worth and taught me to be the head and not the tail or anything in between. He showed me how to keep my self-respect by letting me know I deserve better than I'd had in the past. He says I deserve a man who really loves me and only me. I'm telling my story to help other women who might be in the same situation I was in. Ladies, you need to know that you deserve your own man; accept nothing less.

Having affairs that involve adultery or fornication strips you of your dignity; this lowers your self-respect and damages your self-esteem.

Ladies, when you are in one of these types of affairs, the other party has total control, especially if he is married. You have to follow his schedule, and you can't be seen with him anywhere for fear of someone seeing you unless he's a married man who doesn't respect his wife. If he has a family to support, he can't help you financially. This is another way he controls the relationship, and you deserve better. You deserve to have a relationship with your own man, the way God created it to be, through marriage. So be patient and trust God to see you through. After all, God loves you unconditionally, and he will put a deserving man in your life.

When I was freed from adultery, I was released from the mental bondage I was living in. I was better able to focus on things that were really important, like getting closer to God and living righteously. This transformation opened my mind to accept the things God planned for my life and gave me the freedom to experience God's love.

There is no feeling like the one you experience when God frees you from bondage. It frees your mind, body, and soul! God showers you with his unconditional love and protects you from harm. He accepts you as his child, and you are bound for heaven. *God should be first in your life, and the man you love should want to make you his wife.*

CHAPTER 2
Knowing God

*Knowing God doesn't mean saying all the right things;
your faith has to impact the way you live.*

Most people say they know God, but there's a difference between knowing God personally and knowing about God. I have no doubt that they know of God, but I am uncertain that they really know him. To really know God, you must have faith in him, making a choice to live in the light, obey his word, and do his will, disregarding what you feel, think, and desire.

In Ephesians 4:18, NLT, God says, "Their minds are full of darkness; they wander far from the life God gives because they have closed their minds and hardened their hearts against him." He goes on to say in 1 John 2:39, NLT, "If someone claims, 'I know God,' but doesn't obey God's commandments, that person is a liar and is not living in the truth."

To know God, you have to have a personal relationship with him. It takes genuine humility to have faith in God; you can no longer depend on yourself. You have to trust in his ability and not your own! You must have a close relationship with God, like the one you have with your family. He should be in your everyday life. This relationship with God will develop as you grow and mature in the spirit of God after you get to know him and accept him into your heart. When you activate your belief to obey his word, your attitude toward him will change, and you'll use your intelligence to honor him.

God doesn't want to exist only in your mind; he wants to exist in your heart! When you open your heart to him, it shows that you want to obey and honor him. Having honor motivates faith, and faith is the key to pleasing God. Scripture says we must walk by faith and not by sight, but most of us live in fear of making the right choices. We see evidence of a higher power; however, since we can't put our hands on him, we question if he really exists. Ultimately, we're only going to know God through walking by faith.

The Holy Bible provides proof that God is real, and its words confirm our salvation. We have the opportunity to choose what we believe in. When we think we want the freedom to choose what we want in life rather than making the choice for God that brings freedom, we live in fear and lack faith in the promises that would give us eternal life.

Your faith has to impact the way you live; otherwise, it's meaningless and even offensive. It implies that you don't really have a relationship with God. Below is a saying taken from the book *How to Find God.*

There is an engraving on a cathedral wall in Germany that says:

You call me master, and obey me not
You call me light, and see me not
You call me the way, and walk me not
You call me life, and live me not
You call me fair, and love me not
You call me rich, and ask me not
You call me eternal, and seek me not
If I condemn you, blame me not

This engraving asks, do you really know God? The only way to truly know him is to read the Bible and focus on him. You have to put your priorities in order. They are so powerful that they drive your decisions, and your decisions decide your behavior; your behavior in turn dictates your emotions, which influence your mind. Christians can have a carnal mind-set; these people do what they want to do, living outside of God's will. They satisfy their own desires and live in darkness, disobeying God's word.

To live a blessed life, you have to be a born-again Christian, living righteously and obeying the word of God. There is no way around it! You may not feel ready to give your life to God, but keep in mind that you can't predict your time of passing. I hope you are ready when that time comes.

Just ask yourself this question: If Jesus returns right now, will you be ready? There is no specific time to be prepared; perhaps now is the time to change your life! You have to get to know God and start living your life according to his word so that you will be ready at all times. Knowing God is vitally important, and whether you know God determines your destiny when you leave this world!

CHAPTER 3
God's Will

God's will is for us to live in peace and joy, loving our neighbors
as we love ourselves, representing the love he has for us all.

After I became a born-again Christian, I discovered the real purpose of God's will for me. When God created Adam and Eve, they became one. God planned for them to have eternal life and live happily ever after. But then Satan deceived Eve and brought downfall to man, which created dishonor to God and placed sin on mankind.

In today's world, we are living in a state of dishonor to the point of disobeying and disgracing the word of God by letting two of the most infectious sins destroy the human race. These sins are stopping the blessings people could be receiving. The Bible is one of the best-selling books ever, and it continues to remain at the top of the list. It can be found in almost every household across the nation, but for some reason, it's the least read book. *Everyone might have a Bible, but everyone doesn't read it, even the people who proclaim to be Christians.*

The Bible holds the key for people to have eternal life, but we still don't read it. It carries answers to every problem we might have in our lives. Within its pages are scriptures to set us free, but we still won't apply it to our lives. The Bible is like a bag of seed that you plant in your heart, sowing knowledge into your life to meet all your needs. We just have to do the step of planting the seed (the word of God) to bring forth a harvest *because whatever we sow in our heart, our ears, and our mouth will grow in our minds!*

God says that his people suffer because of a lack of knowledge, and he provides us with the Bible to teach us his word for deliverance, but we still won't read it. The saying goes, if we have the knowledge to know better, we will do better! God gives us knowledge through his word so that we can live happy and blessed lives. In contrast, Jesus says in scripture, "The thief's purpose is to steal and kill and destroy. My purpose is to give them a rich and satisfying life" (John 10:10, NLT).

For those of you who don't read the Bible and don't know what its pages contain, God says you are living in total darkness but walking around believing that you are living right. However, the word of God is his wisdom, and you are living outside the will of God, blocking the blessings he has for your life. When you are not living in the word of God, you're living by the world's system, leaning on your own understanding and doing as you please.

Most people think they are wise, but wisdom means applying knowledge in the right way. Proverbs 4:7 KJV, says, "Wisdom is the principal thing; therefore get wisdom: and with all thy getting get understanding." That means not leaning on your own understanding but on the word of God. When you get wisdom, prosperity lies ahead. God can deliver you into the marvelous light and supply you with the wisdom to recognize the difference, breaking the habits you have that lead you to commit sin.

You have to change your mind-set to one of living righteously. Who you choose to believe in, God or Satan, determines your future. If you are not living in God's world, you are living in Satan's world. Everything good hates everything evil, and vice versa.

You have to make a choice; God says you can't serve two masters, for you will hate one and love the other. You can't have one foot in the world and the other in the kingdom.

When you live as the world does, you are leaning on your own understanding, refusing to obey the word of God. He says that when you disobey his word, your days will be short. You must have faith and trust in God to do what he says he will; he can deliver you out of any problems you are facing. I know this because he delivered me from adultery and fornication. I am forever grateful for his mercy and grace to save my soul! Thank you, Jesus! I give you all the glory and the praise. My life belongs to you!

You must have God in your life to accomplish anything. Faith is the only voice he hears and respects! God feels pain when we doubt him, and he feels pleasure when we believe him. Even with all the success and wealth some of you have, it's nothing without God in your life. We see proof of successful, wealthy people all the time who are not happy; it's because they are missing the number-one ingredient to their happiness, Jesus Christ! He embodies love, and he's the only one who can bring true love and happiness to your life.

In Deuteronomy 8:11, scripture says, "That is the time to be careful! Beware that in your plenty you do not forget the Lord your God and disobey his commands, regulations, and decrees that I am giving you today" (NLT). So don't be deceived, thinking you are responsible for your success. He is the Alpha and the Omega, the first and the last, and no man comes to him, except through his son, Jesus Christ. If you are living an ungodly life and you don't know God, he says you are condemning yourself to destruction. *To have victory in your life, it is necessary to obey God's commandments, do his will, think like he thinks, and say what he says!*

CHAPTER 4
God's Instructions

Failing to take instruction from God gives Satan the power to take what God intended you to have.

God's instructions are very simple: to get his favor, we have to be obedient to his word and have the faith to follow his instructions so we can receive his promises.

I've noticed that in difficult times, people tend to depend on whomever they trust most, even turning to God when things aren't going well. However, when things are going right, they rely on their own abilities and leave God out of the equation. They forget he exists because they think they don't need his instructions or guidance anymore, and they trust in their own instincts. We have to learn to submit to God; submission is part of following his instructions. There are three common reasons we don't follow instructions:

- We are afraid of not having control.
- We are rebellious.
- We are headstrong.

People often do what they already know is wrong. They've been doing it so long that they think it is right. So they rebel against instructions, fearing they're trying to control them; people on this path become headstrong, refuse to do what's right, and disobey the word of God. When you fail to follow God's instructions, Satan has access to stop your blessings. However, when you obey God's instructions by applying them to your life, you receive the blessings he intends for you.

In Matthew 18:3, God says, "Truly I tell you, unless you change and become like little children, you will never enter the kingdom of heaven" (NIV). This instruction is easy to interpret; God is simply saying to humble yourself as you would to your parents, following his instructions and obeying his word, or you will face the consequences.

There are three things you have to do to see God:

- Submit to him.
- Serve him.
- Sow into his kingdom.

We are accountable to a higher authority, and we are able to tell when human laws contradict divine laws established by God; the laws of God surpass manmade laws. We need laws in our lives to build walls of protection. If we don't have these laws, problems and temptations will flood into our lives, attempting to destroy us, but God's word is greater than any troubles we face. We have spiritual protection through the blood of the lamb, and trouble will pass over us; it can't touch us. The Holy Spirit seals us for salvation, but the blood of Jesus saves us! Hallelujah! Thank you, Jesus, for you mercy and grace. Most people are saved but not free; they are still living in bondage because of their disobedience to God's instructions. Doubt is the enemy to God's blessings being manifested for us, so do not doubt the word of God; your life depends on it. Be full of Christ and let him use you for good. Your old nature will try to control you, but your new nature, which is the Holy Spirit, will take over. He gives you the power to resist sin and overcome your sinful nature; this cannot be done in your own strength.

Choosing to obey God's instructions gives you a transition from physical death to eternal life in heaven. Make heaven your choice, by following God's instructions and obeying his word, or hell will be your only option! Where are you headed, heaven or hell?

CHAPTER 5
Satan's Deceit

*Satan's deceit is to make what's wrong look right, using
God's law for his own purpose, with situations like
common-law marriage and prenuptial agreements.*

Satan's primary purpose is to steal, kill, and destroy with any
means necessary. He is called the prince of darkness. He's a master
at deceiving people, and he can show up in any form or fashion!
Satan's responsible for most people living outside the will of God;
he influences people to live disgracefully, as this world does. There
is another world, and it's God's kingdom, which he reigns over.
Let's face it; there is really only one world—that's the one God
created—but Satan makes people think there are two worlds. Most
people are living as this world does; they're doing as they please,
not even acknowledging that God exists! Fortunately for us, God's
standards were established way before Satan intervened.

When Adam and Eve were created, the laws of God's kingdom
were already established. When Satan deceived Eve and she
disobeyed God's word, it brought sin into existence; however,
God's grace saved us from damnation and set us free. With that
freedom, he also gave us a wonderful and dangerous gift called
free will. This gives us the ability to choose between right and
wrong, good and evil, God and Satan, and heaven and hell. God

will not force his salvation and forgiveness upon our lives; it's our place to say yes or no. If anyone ends up in hell, it's because of his or her deliberate decision to reject God's offer of forgiveness.

People in the world today are living in ungodly ways, performing such sins as adultery and fornication. These sins become so popular that they are accepted by society. Both men and women are having extramarital affairs, while others are in relationships with multiple partners. The sad thing about this is that Satan has deceived us into thinking it's acceptable behavior. Well, I have a dose of reality for you: it's wrong, ungodly, and disgraceful.

When Jesus died on the cross, he took us from living disgracefully to living in grace. We have forgotten just how much he suffered for us to be free, for we are still living as this world does, with no morals or values; this is destroying our nation. Satan's success at destroying humankind is affecting us in a big way. People are bailing out of their marriages, abandoning their families, and raising the divorce rates until they're off the charts. We are deceived to the point of applauding ourselves when we commit these acts; people are celebrating their divorces like it's a good thing. Wake up! This is a deception from the devil, and he does not have your best interest in mind.

Satan wants to keep you in darkness because that's where his strength is. He keeps you from the knowledge of God's word, which prevents you from discovering and getting deliverance into eternal life and keeps you in poverty and lack.

The word of God is called the sword of the spirit, and when you are ignorant of his word, you cannot defeat the devil with its great power. In Proverbs 11:9, the Bible says, "With their words, the godless destroy their friends, but knowledge will rescue the righteous" (NLT). Having the knowledge of God's word brings fruit to your life. Therefore, you must not give Satan the upper hand. He only brings destruction!

Satan's so good at deceiving us that he has us believing that marriage is a bad thing. The confirmation of this is the broken marriages and divorces we see every day. However, God created marriage to bring a man and woman together in covenant, vowing to love each other until death. Satan has manipulated us into having common-law marriages, which allow a man and woman to live together outside of matrimony. Common-law marriages are not of God; they are from a manmade law that only exists in Satan's world. This is a form of fornication, which is sin, allowing you to live outside of God's law, which will destroy you.

Satan's deception would have us believe we live only in a visible world—the world we see presently—so we do as the world does. If we believe this, we refuse to see the invisible world, which is God's kingdom, where his laws are established. God gives us a choice to live eternally or to die by disobeying his word and honoring Satan.

We can choose to do now what we will be satisfied with later; that is, we can choose God's way now to receive eternal life later. Wisdom from the Holy Spirit allows us to make choices such as this. We have to make constructive decisions in our lives to receive what God promises us. We also have to start living in love: loving God like he loves us, loving our neighbors like we love ourselves, keeping our marriages together, and helping those in need. These are the things that please God.

We humans are constantly looking for love. Just look up and try God; he is love! When we apply all these things to our lives, we portray the love of God and move from disgrace to grace, destroying the deceptions that Satan has created.

The famous British author C. S. Lewis says, "The gates of hell are locked from the inside," meaning there is no way out! Take heed to this message and turn from your sinful ways to please God. He only honors obedience; his gift is eternal life, and disobedience makes hell your only option!

CHAPTER 6
Covenant in Marriage

*God's covenant is based on agape love, the kind of love
that God portrays for us; it never gives up, never loses
faith, and endures through every circumstance.*

Marriage is a covenant that God created for a man and a woman
to live in commitment to each other until death do they part,
including the performance of a spiritual ceremony to bring them
together as one. Most people are unaware of the spiritual side of
this commitment, due to their lack of biblical knowledge. Most
people seem to know the formality of making these vows, but they
don't understand the significance of what these vows really mean;
even I was guilty of this.

In Hebrews 13:4, God says, "Give honor to marriage, and
remain faithful to one another in marriage. God will surely judge
people who are immoral and those who commit adultery" (NLT).
In Ephesians 5:21–22, God says "Submit to one another out
of reverence for Christ. Wives, submit yourselves to your own
husbands as you do to the Lord" (NIV).

In 1 Corinthians 7:38, God says that a wife is bound to her
husband as long as he lives, and if her husband dies, she is free
to marry anyone else as long as he loves the Lord. If her husband

lives and she remarries, she will be committing adultery. These are laws God established for married people.

The man has always been the head in a marriage, with total authority; however, in most cases, both men and women are stepping out of their marriages and destroying the covenant God created.

When we rely on our feelings of passion, they control our actions to commit these sinful acts. Scripture says in 1 Corinthians 7:36, "But if a man thinks that he's treating his fiancée improperly and will inevitably give in to his passion, let him marry her as he wishes. It is not a sin" (NLT). Acting on your passions can cover a broad range of things, such as kissing passionately, caressing, touching intimately, or even having sexual or oral relations. None of these things should be practiced until you marry that individual, for they are acts of fornication. You should only participate in this behavior with your husband or wife; nothing else is acceptable in the kingdom of God.

Every person will be accountable for his or her actions. If you are having promiscuous affairs with someone you are not married to, you are committing sin. We must stop leaning on our own understanding and doing as we please, disobeying the laws of God. We must focus on his word and on doing his will; he supplies us with the wisdom to know right from wrong.

Hypothetically speaking, let's just say that man made a law where married people could not end their marriages under any circumstances, or else they would face sudden death. I'm sure that they would do everything in their power to make their marriages last. When you think about it, it's almost similar to the laws that God created for marriage. The only difference is that under God's law, you would not be facing sudden death; the death he speaks of allows you to live until a natural death or some unforeseen death occurs between the two of you.

Now isn't it funny that when man enforces a law, you obey it or face the consequences? However, when God gives you a choice his way, you don't take it seriously because he doesn't imply instant death. In all reality, the outcome is still death, whether it is the instant death that man implies when you break the hypothetical covenant, or the death that occurs within your marriage when you obey God's word. It doesn't take a rocket scientist to figure out which choice to make between dying at the hands of Satan—allowing him to deceive you into adultery, fornication, divorce, and separation, destroying the covenant that God created—and obeying God's laws to live eternally.

When we obey God's laws, it pleases him and allows him to manifest his promises to us. As children of God, we cannot continue to allow Satan to deceive humankind and destroy our destiny. Sin is so terrible because it uses God's laws for its own purpose, destroying what God established. Satan has dramatically changed the way God intended us to live, in eternal love and peace. We have to take back our future by putting our faith in God, trusting him to deliver us from all evil, and wiping out all our sins so we can have the life he created for us.

We cannot continue having affairs, dishonoring and destroying the marriage covenant to satisfy our desires. Unfortunately, people have misunderstood that covenant. They make marriage what they want it to be, allowing divorce and separation as a possible solution for their problems. In God's kingdom, these solutions don't exist! They are answers that Satan provides to get us to disobey God's law.

Satan's deception is to make what's wrong look right, but the marriage commitment is very serious; it's not just something to do because we say we love someone. The vows represent committing to someone forever. Love is not just some gooey emotion. In the Greek language, love is described in three different ways: eros (physical attraction), philia (love between friends), and agape (unconditional love)

Marriages that are based on physical attraction alone and those based on love between friends will not survive, because they are not based on unconditional, agape love. Emotions come and go, but true love is more than that; when we marry, we must obey the covenant, taking it very seriously to the point of utmost obedience. It can never be broken under any circumstances except those found in the law of God. You must grasp the sincerity of what a covenant of marriage really means rather than believing what people say a marriage should be.

When we marry someone for material things, it won't last, because the relationship lacks the agape love that we should have for each other—the love that God has for us—and it endures forever! Statistics have proven that problems will occur in these types of marriages; however, when these problems occur, we must not give up at the first sign of trouble. We took vows to be in the marriage until death, and divorce and separation are not God's ways to solve the problem.

You have been misled to believe human solutions are best. You must turn to God when trouble occurs, for he has the answers to all your problems; he is a problem solver! He will take all your burdens and make them his. In Matthew 11:28, God says, "Come to me, all of you who are weary and carry heavy burdens, and I will give you rest" (NLT). He will deliver you out of darkness and into the marvelous light; he loves you that much!

So if you see your marriage on the brink of failure, turn to God; he's got your back. I just wish I had known earlier what I know now. I could have saved my marriage. As the saying by Maya Angelou goes, "When you know better, you do better." We must look for things in our marriages that are relevant and valuable to keep the covenant strong. Once you realize what the covenant stands for, you'll know it doesn't allow anything or anyone to destroy it—not adultery, fornication, separation, or divorce, for these things are not accepted in a covenant committed to God.

There is a famous married couple, Billy Davis Jr. and Marilyn McCoo, singing artists from the group the Fifth Dimension. They have been married for over forty years. I am sure that they have had some experience with the "for better or worse" of life, but they have endured through it all. They have Christ in their lives, so their marriage will last as long as they put God first.

They continue to sing, and now they sing for the Lord. Their example is one illustration that a man and woman can be together in matrimony for as long as their lives continue, as long as God is a part of the marriage. God has to be included in your everyday life whether you're married or single if you wish to have success.

Billy and Marilyn were interviewed on *Praise the Lord*, a spiritual show on TBN Network, in June 2011. They were asked what keeps their marriage together, and they replied that you first need God in your life; you have to be committed to doing the right thing to make your marriage successful. Everything comes with a price. You have to work at anything you do in life to have success, starting with yourself, by acknowledging what you want out of your marriage; it takes the two of you to commit to that.

Marriage is not about finding the right person; it's about being the right person who is willing to commit to God's covenant. If this is true, there should be no problem finding someone to marry. However, people tend to let what they feel outweigh what God wants. They operate in the flesh, allowing sin to manifest in their lives.

In all marriages, couples vow to love each other, but in some marriages they end up hating each other somehow. We have to change that concept and prevent this deception of Satan from destroying our families. Our success lies in God's hand, be it within our marriages, our finances, our health, or any other problems we are faced with.

There are three things that cause problems in our marriages: communication problems, sex, and money. If we can solve these three areas in our marriages, we will be on our way to success! However, we can't do this without God. Communication problems are one of the main reasons marriages fail. First and foremost, if there is no communication, there is no room for change. If you can't talk about your problems, how do you expect to solve them? You must be able to sit down and talk about what's going on in your marriage, or it is likely headed for failure.

There is a common conception that most men don't like talking. But if he is a real man and a godly man who cares about his family, then there shouldn't be a problem. If these things aren't important to him, then he shouldn't be married. Repairing communication problems is the most important part to salvaging a troubled marriage.

Communication is the pipeline to discussing and solving the problems that your marriage may be experiencing; it's the lifeline that will give the marriage a chance to survive. It gives both parties a chance to find the source of the problem and allows both parties to discuss the matters and solve the problems together. If for some reasons one of you doesn't want to communicate, the marriage will not survive.

Sex is an important part of a marriage, but it should not surpass the focus you give to your love for each other. You both should express your needs to each other and learn each other's desires so that you can both experience satisfaction.

Sex seems to play a great part in a marriage. It has been a primary reason why many marriages fail, but it should not be the reason a marriage fails. In all reality, marriages that are based on sex only will fail anyway, because we should marry for love. Sex and money should only be benefits of the marriage, not the primary reason for a marriage. Sex is a part of the love you have for each other, to provide you both with satisfaction for your sexual needs. God says he gave us sex to be performed between a husband and a wife, for them to please each other. It should not be a reason to destroy the marriage; the relationship should be based on agape love, as mentioned earlier. God's love, which lasts forever, never gives up and endures through any circumstances.

Most people today use sex freely, as if it's a commodity to foster their relationships. They make it a primary reason to have a relationship, but the love two people have for each other is what should be the primary reason for a relationship. People should not have relationships based on sex; doing this robs them of their dignity and the respect they should have for themselves.

Wouldn't you like to know that you deserve better by becoming someone's husband or wife and not just a trophy to satisfy someone's desires? When we use sex in this unhealthy manner, we allow ourselves to be cheated out of a worthy relationship. You should focus on becoming someone's companion by having a committed relationship that will lead to marriage the way God created it to be.

Last but not least of these problem areas is money. They say the love of money is the root of all evil. I'm convinced this is true because most people will do *anything* for the love of money. Some people really need it, and some people abuse it.

It has taken the number-one spot in destroying all types of relationships, including marriages, friendships, and families. In some marriages, people make money their primary reason to marry someone. The love of money has taken over the love we should have for each other. In Ecclesiastes 5:10, God says, "Those who love money will never have enough. How meaningless to think that wealth brings true happiness" (NLT). The more money you have, the more people come to help you spend it, so what good is wealth, except to watch it slip through your fingers? Money has taken over what God intended money to be used for, to supply our needs! It does not bring true happiness.

Man has used money for greedy purposes and illegal methods, and this is destroying mankind. Money should not be the reason a marriage fails, but in today's society, it is one of the primary reasons most marriages fail. When prenuptial agreements were created for marriages between wealthy people, it was a law made by man to divide the assets between husband and wife. In God's kingdom, no such law applies; husband and wife share everything as one, and this applies to all marriages.

Married couples should come together to manage their money for the needs of the family and not separate it. It's considered our money, not yours or mine. Anything you accumulate in a marriage is for the both of you. There is no separation of anything; you are one! In most households, the man should be the head of the house. There are single-parent homes, where one of the spouses is absent; but in the homes that include a man, he should support the family.

The economy has forced the woman to help provide financial support, and she should have her husband's back to give him the support he needs. No one should be complaining or pointing fingers when trouble occurs; you should be communicating to solve whatever problems you have together. When you can't solve them, go to Jesus Christ for your answers, trusting him to show you the way. He will give you the wisdom and knowledge to do the right thing.

Money is needed for survival. In some cases, having money makes life so much easier. Having money can make or break you. In the world today, it is often a tool to accomplish goals or meet needs. Unfortunately, most of us don't have as much money as we would like. On the other hand, there are those of us who have an abundance of money; those people are not necessarily happy though. We have observed that money doesn't bring happiness. People with money who are sick can buy health care, but they can't buy good health or a cure for their sickness if one doesn't exist.

Fortunately, we have a Savior who can supply all our needs. He can bring us total happiness if we believe and accept him into our hearts to receive the blessed life. Don't let money be an issue that destroys your marriage.

When God created marriage, he wanted all marriages to be successful. We are blessed to have God's love, which never gives up. Without it, we are doomed to let Satan destroy us. Having the love of God in our marriages gives us the ability to beat Satan at his own game!

CHAPTER 7
Adultery

Adultery is the topic of one of the Ten Commandments.
It's tearing down the walls of matrimony that
God created and destroying families.

Now that you have gotten an overall view of God's will for us and his laws for covenant in a marriage, I would like to expose the infectious sin of adultery. This sin is infecting the minds of men and women and causing marriages to fail. It destroys families and breaks down the walls of matrimony that God created.

When I was having my adulterous affair, I knew it was wrong, but I continued to do it. The Bible says that's leaning on your own understanding, refusing to obey the word of God. Aside from my adulterous affair, I felt I was good person, always treating people the way I wanted to be treated. I was kindhearted and giving, helping others in need, and treating people with respect. I felt all my good deeds were my ticket to heaven, but I soon found out that the good things I did would not get me to heaven; the sin I was committing would send me to hell! Heaven is free of sin, and hell is full of sin; that's why they're separated. No one can enter into God's kingdom with sin; sinful people are forbidden to even enter God's presence, for he is pure and holy.

It doesn't matter how many good deeds you do or how much

you go to church. If you are sinning and you don't repent and accept Jesus Christ as your Lord and Savior, your ticket to heaven is null and void! God says that we all have sinned, and we were born into sin, but then he sent his son, Jesus Christ, to save our souls, which freed us from all sin. Hallelujah! Thank you, Jesus, for your grace! God set a system for us to follow; when we obey his word, he gives us everything we need to be successful.

Romans 1:20 says, "For ever since the world was created, people have seen the earth and sky. Through everything God made, they can clearly see his invisible qualities—his eternal power and divine nature. So they have no excuse for not knowing God" (NLT). People always see what they want to see, but the evidence always shows up. When you choose to commit sin, you are suppressing the truth to instead do as you please, believing that it's the right thing to do.

We only see what's visible, which is constantly presenting us with ways to disobey God's word. We must repent and renew our minds to obey the word of God. No man lives forever, and we will be accountable for the way we live; we have to acknowledge the fact that God is the greater power! He exists, and he created the Holy Bible, our guide to righteous living.

Do you know that the way you live determines the way you die? In Romans 6:23, God says, "For the wages of sin is death, but the free gift of God is eternal life through Christ Jesus our Lord" (NLT). The gift of eternal life comes through living a godly life and displaying the love that Christ has for us in the way we act toward others.

When we commit a sin such as adultery, it destroys our homes and families, which leads to the destruction of the nation! It is so important that we make constructive decisions in our relationships and ask God's help to overcome our weaknesses before we commit ourselves to each other.

Let's take marriage vows as an example. We go before a pastor and say our vows, confessing our intent to be together until death. These are very serious vows, and I think people, including myself, have taken these vows very lightly. We are really committing to be with someone forever, with whatever troubles may occur in the marriage. It sounds to me like there should be no way out. It's the ultimate commitment, and it can't be terminated at any cost except through the laws that God applies.

Scripture says, "Love never gives up, never loses faith, is always hopeful, and endures through every circumstance" (1 Cor 13:7, NLT). Can we say we really know the true meaning of love? I think not. We definitely don't portray the love that God describes, as seen by the numerous broken marriages, divorces, and separations.

If we portrayed God's love, divorce and excuses for broken marriages would not exist. Yet the divorce rates are off the charts because we do not love the way we should. We love the way man does, marrying for reasons like money, status, power, and lust. When we marry for any reason other than the love that God describes, our marriages will fail; we see proof of this every day.

When God created Adam and Eve, it was for the purpose of love and companionship. Just as Satan deceived Eve, he's still deceiving humankind today, persuading us to make destructive decisions. When Eve was deceived and chose to sin, humankind was cursed, which changed our ability to have the eternal life God planned for us. However, his grace gives us another chance for a better life. God says in John 10:10 that he comes to bring us life, and bring it more abundantly.

I would like to take some time to talk to the ladies who are having adulterous affairs. These types of affairs strip you of your dignity and self-respect and damage your self-esteem. I know this because I was a victim of this type of relationship. You deserve to have a healthy relationship with a man who loves you and wants to marry you. God created you to be the only woman for a man. He says you should be treated like a queen in a relationship, for your body is a temple, and it is not to be disrespected or unloved! So don't settle for second best, and do not get caught in a dreaded love triangle. That kind of relationship is not healthy; it will destroy you and tear down your confidence. You have to believe you deserve better, be confident in who you are, and carry yourself with pride, knowing that God loves you and wants the best for you.

You have to have faith and trust God for your needs. He will see you through any situations you might be facing and give you the strength to endure any trials. After all, God loves you like no man will. If you need to have a man, God says it's better to marry than to commit sin, so seek to find a husband who is not already married to another woman. That's a sin, and it will invite destruction into your life because it's not accepted by God. For you women who are living with a man out of matrimony, get out or get married. You are committing sin, and God doesn't condone this behavior. A common-law marriage is a deception that's setting you up for damnation.

Sometimes we women give in to certain situations to have or keep a man. I have been there too; it happens out of fear of being lonely or to fulfill immediate lustful desires. This is also true for men. However, God can fill the emptiness created by these wants. He puts other things in your lives, like his word. When you obey God's word, you can do his will, for he says you can do all things through Christ that strengthen you. He will replace your bad habits with the Holy Spirit, which will guide you on the right path; you just have to be patient and wait on God. He wants you to have a man; women were created to be companions for men. Just know that God is faithful, and his love endures forever. When he does send your man, it will be for a lifetime.

I have observed that most people who indulge in adultery think it's harmless. They follow the ways of this world because that's what the majority of people are doing. Many people view adultery as sinless, but it is the topic of one of the Ten Commandments, and its penalty is death! Adultery may seem right, but that's a deception of the devil, and it's destroying our marriages. Because of this, we treat marriage as if it's taboo or it's an artificial institution. However, God created marriage, and nothing he creates is bad.

By changing the way we think, we can change the course of our destiny and destroy Satan's stronghold. I know that this might be hard if you are used to doing things as this world does and you have formed bad habits that are hard to break. However, God will give you the strength to face your fears and break those bad habits.

In some marriages, trouble such as money matters or a lack of communication or intimacy has already manifested; adultery was not the initial cause for problems. When this happens, it leaves room for a third party to enter the situation and for sin to intervene if the spouses are not cautious. This is where both parties should sit down and resolve to fix the problem, talking and getting an understanding of each other's views on the matter. This is very important to solving the problem, and it's the first step to a healing process.

When Eve allowed a third party to intervene and let Satan deceive her to disobey God's instructions, it brought downfall to mankind. Let this be a lesson to you not to let others interfere in your marriage; marriage is supposed to be between one man, one woman, and God. Be careful to not let family and friends cause trouble between the two of you; this can harm your marriage.

Keep God in your marriage, and it will be successful. Now I know that my marriage failed because God wasn't in it. God created marriage, so he should be part of it. The Bible teaches that the key to a successful marriage is putting God first and loving your spouse with agape love, which never gives up and endures through any circumstances. Let's not allow adulterous affairs to continue to destroy the covenant God created. Let's take back our families and focus on our destinies so that we can have the promises of God. Let's be happily married until death do us part, the way God created it to be.

CHAPTER 8
Fornication

This sin is sending a message that having multiple relationships is acceptable. In God's kingdom, this is called sexual immorality, and it's forbidden!

Fornication is another sin that's destroying the dignity of mankind. It's another deception from the devil. This sin runs so rampant in our society that it's actually ruining all chances of relationship survival. It has destroyed the respect men and women have for each other. Fornication is like a fad that is out of control, and it's causing major problems in our society, including unprotected sex, disease, fatherless homes, and teenage parents. Because these situations are so common, people believe that having multiple relationships outside of marriage is the thing to do.

However, it's another big sin, and it's called sexual immorality. Sex is only supposed to be between a husband and wife, and if God were judging people today, most of us would be doomed! But thank God for his grace and mercy that saved our souls, giving us a chance to change our lives.

Promiscuity is a form of fornication; it's when men and women have relations with anyone they please. This sin destroys your self-respect and your dignity, eventually causing your downfall.

God only honors marriage; he doesn't condone promiscuous

behavior. This disobedient behavior causes destruction in your life. God loves you so much that he gives you the chance to change your lifestyle by repenting your sins and starting to live righteously after accepting him into your heart. In your relationships, you have to commit to contemplating marriage; if you are not ready to marry, it does not give you a reason to sow your wild oats everywhere. I had affairs that included fornication and sowing my oats, but I repented my sins and accepted God in my life, and he freed me. He wiped all my sins away, never to be seen again! I thank him every day for his mercy and grace that saved my soul!

It's vital that when you're making a choice to seek a significant other that you look for a commitment from him or her; otherwise, you will be in a position of disobedience. In today's world, most people look for companions for the wrong reasons. When they should be looking for a husband or wife, they tend to look to fulfill their immediate desires, whatever that might be: money, sex, material things, or an escape from loneliness. When most men look for a woman, they look at outside appearances, wanting her to be sexy and pretty and to have a nice body. Men may look for these things, but they must do so with the right intention of finding a wife and should consider other traits they might want her to have.

The Bible says, "The man who finds a wife finds a treasure, and he receives favor from the Lord" (Prv 18:22, NLT). Women weren't meant to be flings or people to fulfill your immediate desires. You have to look beyond the physical appearance to see the heart of a woman; find out if she's wife material and if she's pure and genuine. God looks at us as complete people and into our hearts; our physical appearance doesn't move him. Start looking for a woman you desire for her worth, and you might just find a wife.

Some men and women just want casual relationships. Why is this? Could it be because we don't want committed relationships or responsibilities or because we don't trust each other? Trust is a very important part of a relationship, and if you don't have it, your relationship won't last. God created men and women to be together, and this can only happen if we love and trust each other. We are going to have responsibilities in our lives no matter what; however, the responsibility should become lighter when there are two people there to share it within a relationship. We can't let Satan destroy what men and women should be to each other: honest, trustworthy, and responsible adults; we counteract Satan's schemes in this area through forming committed relationships.

A woman wants a man who loves her and wants her to be his wife, the way God created it to be. We must stop being deceived by Satan. We should be in committed relationships as husbands and wives. Some people may think there is no fun to living this way, but this is because they are used to their sinful ways of doing things. The devil has taken away what God established marriage to be and destroyed God's law.

Some people say that having multiple relationships is just the nature of men. I don't know what men's nature is supposed to be or what men think their nature should be; in God's kingdom, that nature doesn't exist. Practicing fornication is following the ways of this world. No human is above God. He created men, and he can destroy them! To the men living by your egos and believing that your behavior proves your manhood, you are mistaken and leaning on your own understanding. When God created you, he created you a man, and that's your proof right there. Your proof is not in bragging about how many women you can get as you have promiscuous affairs.

What you think makes you a man is not what God says makes you a man. You have to humble yourself before God. The Bible says that a humble man submits to God's will regarding what he thinks, feels, and sees. It takes genuine humility to have faith in God and depend on his power, not your own ability. Men, you must submit to God and be the man he created you to be. This happens through displaying the fear of God and showing him that you can be a man of dignity by having a healthy relationship with a woman you want to make your wife and not being promiscuous. Men who are applauded for promiscuous behavior are actually being set up by Satan for damnation.

Women have faults too; they tend to seek a man for worldly possessions or material things, using their bodies to get what they want. I know this because I've been there too. However, when God created each of our bodies, it was supposed to be a holy temple for our husbands only, not to be enjoyed by other men. Thank God I have been delivered from that!

I desperately want to reach out to women who are where I once was, to help them become free and to experience the love of God. All you men and women who are having multiple relationships, living as this world does, you are choosing your destiny and condemning yourselves to honor Satan by committing sin. No matter how good you are in this world, you're going to have to live beyond your feelings and recognize that God has given you the knowledge to know right from wrong. You can choose who you want to serve, God or Satan.

When you are making that choice between God's way and Satan's, you have to make it without involving your feelings; sometimes it's your feelings that get you in trouble. You have to use the wisdom God gave you. Your feelings can be demanding, but you must learn to control them instead of letting them control you. Managing your feelings gives you a sense of independence. They play a big part in our lives; most of the time, they influence how you react to certain situations. Let me use myself as an example. When I was having my adulterous affairs, I knew what I was doing was wrong, but I chose to do it anyway. I let my feelings overrule my judgment as I continued these affairs, overlooking the fact that it was wrong. I let my feelings manage me; I didn't manage them.

We, as people, often rely on our feelings and refuse to face the reality of a situation, and we let those feelings control us. God gave us wisdom and the ability to choose between what's right and wrong; our sinful nature is the source of the problem.

However, you will never master sin and live a life pleasing to God of your own ability; apart from God you can do nothing! God wants us to have happy and healthy relationships whether we are married or single; however, we must conduct them according to his standards.

If you are single, you have to abide by the commitment to consider marriage in your relationships and obey God's word. Marriage is God's creation, and we have to show persistence in obeying his covenant. If we are not persistent, fornication takes control of our passions and increases our desires to use each other.

Society uses women's sexuality to sell everything from toothpaste to automobiles. Women sometimes objectify themselves, using their bodies as means of survival. However, your body belongs to God, and he created it to be a holy temple that is loved and respected, not a drop-off point for men to satisfy their immediate needs.

Men, you should treat women as God says, as a prized possession. Show her love and respect, and love her as you love yourself. It's unfortunate that the younger generation disrespects women, calling them all sorts of names that lower their self-esteem and challenge their womanhood. We as a society have allowed this to happen. We must counteract this by teaching our sons to love and respect women and let men know that women were created as companions who will make them happy.

Women, don't lower yourselves to please a man. You're only supposed to be submissive to him if he's your husband. If you are with someone who's asking you to be sexually immoral and he's not your husband, just tell him that since he won't go to heaven with you, you can't go to hell with him, and get out of the relationship, especially if he won't marry you.

The only way you're going to get out of sin is by accepting Jesus as your Lord and Savior, obeying God's word, and doing his will; this will destroy the playground that Satan created in your life.

CHAPTER 9
God's Power within Us

God's power within us enables us to be just like Christ through his gift of the Holy Spirit, giving us the power to overcome all sin.

When Jesus was crucified, he was resurrected on the third day and now sits on the right hand of God. Everyone who believes will be saved, and anyone who doesn't believe will be condemned. These statements are widely accepted in Christianity. Scripture says that we, the righteous ones, possess the same powers of Jesus Christ and we must believe that we have them without a shadow of a doubt. In Matthew 17:20, Jesus says, "I tell you the truth, if you had faith even as small as a mustard seed, you could say to this mountain, 'Move from here to there,' and it would move" (NLT). Therefore, in order to use such power, our faith must not waver.

When God created the heavens and the earth, he was the architect; he created all people from one man. The purpose of his creation was to draw people close to himself. His ability is so far beyond what we can imagine that his power is considered supernatural. We humans don't have the intelligence to fully comprehend the manifestations of God's power. As a believer, you will experience the power of God by the faith and trust you have in him. The gift of the Holy Spirit is within you; he has the powers to overcome anything you face in life. He will remove all fear and put your enemies under your feet. Jesus's resurrection freed you from all failures, giving you freedom from all the sickness, poverty, and bondage caused by Satan.

You have to constantly wear the whole armor of God, described in Ephesians 6, and be prepared for any spiritual warfare you are faced with. Wearing your spiritual armor at all times gives you the power to have victory over Satan's attacks and temptations. When you are facing spiritual warfare, it may seem like there is no way out; you must stand with strength and fearlessness, withstanding any trials you face. God's power can overcome any obstacles you face and destroy all strongholds that Satan confronts you with! You just have to believe.

We have the power in our tongues to speak things into our lives. We have to be careful how we speak, for what we say manifests into our lives. When you speak with the intention to seek revenge on people who have abused you, this same abuse may come back on you. Your speech must not be harmful of others, for you will reap what you sow. Behave like Jesus and ask for forgiveness for those who have abused you, leaving your problems in God's hand. Romans 12:19 says, "Vengeance is mine; I will repay, saith the Lord" (KJV).

In Proverbs 18:21, God says, "The tongue can bring death or life; those who love to talk will reap the consequences" (NLT). This scripture indicates the power you have within you, telling you whatever comes out of your mouth will exist in your life. Therefore, don't speak harshly of yourself or others.

In Luke 10:19, God says, "Look, I have given you authority over all the power of the enemy, and you can walk among snakes and scorpions and crush them. Nothing will injure you" (NLT). When you are a believer and trust in God as your Lord and Savior, you have access to God's supernatural powers. We have the power to wipe out Satan's deception regarding adultery and fornication, behaviors that are tempting men and women to destroy the foundation of marriage that God established. By exercising these powers, we will destroy the stronghold that Satan has on our people as we help eliminate the prevalence of the sins that are leading to our nation's destruction.

CHAPTER 10
Promises of God

God's word is his promise, and it's sharper than a two-edged sword, cutting between soul and spirit, joint and marrow (Heb 4:12).

When we do what God desires, it's one of the greatest investments we could make in our lives. Being obedient to God brings his promises into existence. God's promises are forever, and his word is his bond.

God's word is a standard of his holiness; it sets laws for us to follow and brings forth his promises, as mentioned previously. We must live sin-free lives to receive these promises; it's not God's will for a believer to fall into sin. If we miss the mark, we must repent and conform to God's word. If we don't, the presence of sin in our lives will break our fellowship with God and give Satan the opportunity to harass us.

Jesus's blood saves us from all of our troubles and cleanses us from condemnation! If we continue to sin, we will be condemning ourselves. Hebrews 10:26 says, "Dear friends, if we deliberately continue sinning after we have received knowledge of the truth, there is no longer any sacrifice that will cover these sins" (NLT). If we continue to disobey God's word, we are refusing to honor his laws. We, as believers, should be forever thankful for God's grace, his unconditional love, and his promise to give us eternal life.

My pastor, Bishop Henry Fernandez, said at one of his Sunday morning services, "Cast all your cares on God, for trouble doesn't last always. God is always in control; he's always a step ahead, and victory is on the way. If you don't believe, you will never experience the greatness of God."

God's word guarantees his promises are true. We will never attain success in our lives without studying God's word. God has put a gift in each one of us, but we often pursue our passions instead of the gifts God gives us. I always tried to get ahead by doing everything I thought would make me successful, and I didn't acknowledge that God had given me a gift. I was so busy trying to pursue things on my own, and I constantly failed. God's power is greater than any success we dream of. We may not all become famous pursuing our passions, but we have to pursue the gifts that God puts within us.

If for some reason you don't know what your gift is, look at it this way: it's whatever you do best and with the least amount of effort! Let God do a work in you, showing you what gifts you have and using you as a vessel to exercise your gift in his kingdom. The whole purpose behind your gift is to help others in need and spread God's word all over the world, bringing those in darkness into his peaceful rest. Hebrews 4:1 says, "God's promise of entering his rest still stands, so we ought to tremble with fear that some of you might fail to experience it" (NLT).

On his television program, Pastor Joel Osteen from Lakewood Church in Houston, Texas, has his congregation recite the following before each sermon:

This is my Bible; I am what it says I am.

I have what it says I have.

I can do what it says I can do.

Today I will be taught the word of God.

I boldly confess: my mind is alert; my heart is receptive.

I will never be the same.

These are powerful words that represent the promises of God. The first line says, "I am who I say I am." In the Bible, God says we are his children, the righteousness of God. The second line says, "I have what it says I have." God says, as righteous ones, we can have anything in his name we ask for; we must seek him first and all these things will be given to us. The third line says "I can do what it says I can do." God says you can do all things through Christ who strengthens you. The fourth line says, "I will be taught the word of God," and God says to honor and obey his word by placing it in your heart. The fifth line says, "I boldly confess my mind is alert and my heart is receptive." God says that you are forever changed when your mind is alert and focused on him and your heart is receptive to obey his word. Pastor Joel Osteen knows that these are God's promises, and he is teaching his church the word of God so that they will know God's love.

God's promises are based solely on faith as we know and obey his word. When we make a promise to someone, we can't go back on our word; we can't break it. God is faithful to keep his word to an even greater degree, for his faithfulness endures forever. He is holy and pure, and he loves us very much!

We know that God's agape love for us endures forever. How many human beings can truly say they love with the type of love that God has for us? Truthfully, not one! This kind of love requires total commitment to someone. Not many people, if any, will commit to someone forever. Our marriages, friendships, and relationships prove every day that we humans do not carry that kind of love in our nature. However, God knows that our flesh is very weak and we are easily influenced by the desires of this world, so he sent us the Holy Spirit to give us the strength to overcome our weaknesses.

We will always need God to see us through our circumstances, but we must start loving the way he does. Only then will we be able to love without fear. Just imagine it; if we had love for each other like God has for us, we would have a world of happiness and joy. We could wipe out all the diseases that plague our nation. We would conquer unforgiveness, hatred, deceit, jealousy, and envy. Our families would stay together with no need for child support, no teenage pregnancies, no homosexuality, no sickness, no adultery, and no fornication or any other bondage that weakens us. In summary, living in agape love will destroy the deceit of Satan that dwells among us and confirm our victory as conquerors through Jesus Christ.

CHAPTER 11
From Disgrace to Grace

God's grace gives us the power to live a life pleasing to him, so let's stop honoring Satan by living in disgrace.

Let me start off by saying we can have heaven right here on earth. In the Lord's Prayer, there is a phrase that says, "Thy will be done on earth, as it is in heaven" (Mt 6:10, KJV). It also says in scripture that whatever God binds on earth, he binds in heaven (Mt 18:18). God intended for us to live in a state of heaven on earth, but when we die, it's our souls that will travel to heaven or hell. If you want to go to heaven, you have to be living a righteous life, obeying God's word, and doing his will, for obedience is the key to kingdom living.

Jesus was crucified on the cross to save our souls. It was a gift from God, which freed us from all sin. Unfortunately, we have forgotten his grace and exactly what it implies. Jesus suffered complete separation from God in our place so that we wouldn't have to. We must stop giving Satan honor in our lives by having no love for each other, stealing from and killing each other, destroying our marriages, and having promiscuous affairs. If we stop and think about the way we are living, we're giving Satan honor through our actions. We must start honoring God by changing our mind-sets to love each other the way God loves us. When we do this, we will magnify his name by honoring his ways.

Disobedience brings a death sentence and will prevent you from entering heaven if you don't repent. However, God has the power to help you overcome the temptation to sin, and he can turn your wrongs to right. Anything is possible with God. Stop carrying envy, jealousy, and unforgiveness in your heart; these are things that will set you apart from God. He asks, "How can you love me and not love your neighbor or show love for others?"

We destroy the commitment we made to keep our marriages together by giving up when trouble occurs even though the vows say "until death do us part"!

God says, "You must love the Lord your God with all your heart, all your soul, and all your mind.' This is the first and greatest commandment. A second is equally important: 'Love your neighbor as yourself'" (Mt 22:38–39). If for some reason you don't love yourself, get to know God on a personal level so that he can instill within you his love for you. This will inspire you to love others. We show love for each other by helping others in need, wiping out diseases that are destroying our nation, and eliminating the ways of Satan that are causing us to sin.

We are tempted to sin when we feel condemned, guilty, rejected, or unloved. God's grace empowers us. In 2 Corinthians 5:17, God says, "Therefore if any man be in Christ, he is a new creature: old things are passed away; behold, all things are become new" (KJV). We no longer have to feel condemned by sin, because Jesus paid the price for us. We are the righteousness of God, and his grace gives us the power to live a life that pleases him. Our salvation is not our doing; it's only by the grace of God that we are saved. So no man can boast about his salvation. The Greek description of grace is "the divine influence upon the heart, and its refection in life," meaning it can be seen in the life of a believer. Grace enables us not to sin.

When God gave us his grace, it enabled us to change our mind-sets to live righteously. However, we are creatures of habit, and sometimes when we are vulnerable, we find ourselves slipping into sin. The Holy Spirit will help us to overcome and endure any temptations we're faced with. We are faced with the influences of this world, but we must not fear the trials we go through, for they strengthen our faith. *All we have to do is trust God and stand strong against our adversaries.*

God has given us a spirit of strength; we don't have to fear, for we are conquerors through him. We will be victorious, for we are the righteousness of God. Honor the grace he's given you by exercising faith in him and finding his deliverance from all transgressions!

God's grace is sufficient to overcome spiritual warfare; with his grace, we are able to defeat the evils of this world on every level. The devil has no defense against a child of God who knows the power of grace. Ephesians 6:10–11 says, "Be strong in the Lord and in his mighty power. Put on all of God's armor so that you will be able to stand firm against all strategies of the devil" (NLT).

God cannot give his grace to proud people, because they believe that they can do things in their own effort. In 1 Peter 5:5–6, the Bible says, "'God opposes the proud but favors the humble.' So humble yourselves under the mighty power of God, and at the right time he will lift you up in honor" (NLT). It pleases God when we trust in him. We do this through honoring his word, doing his will, moving from disgrace to grace in our lifestyles, and giving him all the glory and the praise for the grace he has given us.

CHAPTER 12
Deliverance

To be delivered, we must be born-again Christians, having accepted Jesus as our Lord and Savior, and honoring his word and obeying his laws. We must be submitted to him, serving him, and sowing to him and his kingdom.

This is my final chapter, so I would like to talk to the Christians and the gentiles. For our purposes, a gentile is a person who's not born again. When I became a born-again Christian, God removed the blinders from my eyes. I was once blind, but now I see. I have observed that Christians are sometimes as bad as gentiles.

Now, I know what to expect from the gentiles, but I am unclear about the Christians' motives. I see Christians who claim to be saved but are committing sins. They come to church every Sunday, whooping and hollering and praising God's name, but they harbor jealousy, unforgiveness, envy, and resentment and commit sins that include adultery and fornication. This shows that they are not applying God's word to their lives; they are just hearing the word and taking no action. They are living carnally and not spiritually. Carnal Christians live and do as they please, leaning on their own understanding and disobeying the laws of God, and therefore dishonoring the way he says we should live.

Spiritual Christians obey the word of God. They apply his

word to their everyday life, they have Christlike actions, and they seek more of God and less of themselves. On his November 9, 2011, television broadcast, Pastor Creflo Dollar from Atlanta, Georgia, said there are three stages to spiritual maturity, and you won't mature until you read the Bible and apply it to your life.

- The babysitting stage: Where you are innocent and all sins have been wiped away.
- The childhood stage: Where you are tossed to and fro, having unsteadiness and unreliability, not knowing what God's plan is for you, trying to find yourself.
- The manhood stage: Where you put God first, before yourself, and his word comes before anything; you have the fear of God, pursuing holiness and a pure heart.

Pastor Dollar also says you must seek the kingdom of God first and his righteousness, and all things will be handed unto you. He goes on to say that God's system works by exchange; you must be obedient, for this is the biggest key to releasing God's ability in your life. He says God's love is unconditional, but the promises of God are conditional. Deliverance comes at a price.

Pastor John P. Hagee from St. Louis, Missouri, explained on his October 31, 2011, television program that there are seven steps to being delivered:

- Be a born-again Christian.
- Confess all your sins.
- Denounce the devil.
- Call upon the name of the Lord.
- Forgive anyone who offends you.
- Receive and keep your deliverance through obedience to the word of God.
- Keep a constant relationship with Jesus Christ.

When you apply these seven steps, it guarantees total

deliverance into God's kingdom; the promises of God are a lifetime warranty. Your faith will manifest your deliverance, and that is not easily done; it requires submitting yourself to be humble and obedient and having self-control.

We have to constantly activate our faith through prayer; when we pray in faith, we will have God's attention. Prayer overrides the enemy and activates God to manifest our needs to bring forth a harvest. You've heard the saying, "Prayer changes things." Well, prayer is the only thing that summons God into the earthly realm. Prayer engages what God says and manifests what he promises, and when we don't pray, we allow Satan to intervene in our lives to do what he pleases.

Satan knows that when we don't pray, he has the upper hand! *Prayer is the only weapon that will destroy Satan's kingdom.* God says in Isaiah 54:17, "No weapon that is formed against thee shall prosper; and every tongue that shall rise against thee in judgment thou shalt condemn. This is the heritage of the servants of the Lord, and their righteousness is of me, saith the Lord" (KJV).

We are the righteousness of God, and this means we can't fail; it enables us to obey God and live a fruitful life. Satan cannot harm us in any way; however, we have to be true Christians to receive this blessing.

Now let's just analyze what it takes to be a true Christian. We first have to be born again, accepting Christ as our Lord and Savior, having faith in him, and believing he died to save our souls! We have to talk like God talks, walk like God walks, pursue a pure heart, and stop carrying unforgiveness, jealousy, envy, deceit, and hatred in our hearts. To be a true Christian, we must be just like him. Scripture says, "Be ye holy; for I am holy" (1 Peter 1:16, KJV).

Unfortunately, this cannot be done in our own ability. We need the grace of God, for the flesh is very weak; we can't overcome anything without God.

Being a true Christian is not just going to church every Sunday, praising God, giving tithes, singing in the choir, or being on the usher board; it goes a lot deeper than that. We must have self-control to honor and obey God's word and wear the whole armor of God, using prayer as our weapon to resist the enemy and consistently reading our Bibles to learn the word of God. *We must walk by faith and not by sight to receive the promises of God, for faith is the only way to receive God's grace.*

We have the ability to do anything in life, for God's grace will supply all our needs. True Christians portray the love of God in their everyday life by helping others in need, loving their neighbors like themselves, and spreading the word of God everywhere they go. They acknowledge the power of God to help them endure any trials they face in life through faith in him to access his grace.

Second Peter 1:5 says, "In view of all this, make every effort to respond to God's promises. Supplement your faith with a generous provision of moral excellence, and moral excellence with knowledge, and knowledge with self-control, and self-control with patient endurance, and patient endurance with godliness, and godliness with brotherly affection, and brotherly affection with love for everyone. The more you grow like this, the more productive and useful you will be in your knowledge of our Lord Jesus Christ" (NLT).

So, brothers and sisters, work hard to prove that you are really among those whom God has chosen. A true Christian must abide by God's word and do his will. You can't go around hating each other. You have to release that poison from your system. To become Christlike, you can't carry envy and deceit in your heart.

As true Christians, we have to love one another. We have to walk with pride and dignity, carrying ourselves in a manner that shows we are in the light. We must help those who are in darkness to change their mind-sets to line up with the word of God, helping bring them into the glorious kingdom of eternal life.

You may say you are a Christian, but are you really? If you are, you can't just talk the talk; you have to walk the walk. Verbally expressing your spirituality does not move God, but your actions will get his attention! To be a true Christian, you must back up the words you speak by exercising your faith in God to do his will and receive his grace. It also takes honoring him, lifting up his name, and pursuing holiness to become the Christian he called you to be.

On his television program, Pastor Creflo Dollar said there are five ways for us to obtain our deliverance.

- We need to start reading the Bible to learn God's word, which supplies us with success.
- We need to keep our families together, which includes both a father and a mother.
- We have to teach our children the ways of God and keep them grounded for future success.
- We have to come together in love to save our nation, which is self-destructing.
- We have to wipe out Satan's deception of adultery and fornication. These sins are tempting our men and women to destroy the foundation of marriage that God established.

Our deliverance is at risk! We must honor these instructions by obeying the word of God, saving our nation from escalating to a level of destruction; our salvation depends on it.

I'm hoping that *From Disgrace to Grace* brings a revelation to you, helping you acknowledge the word of God and delivering you out of darkness into God's marvelous light and into his glorious kingdom. Just believe that with God, all things are possible, and you are on your way to salvation. May God bless you all. Amen!

THE HEAVENLY SANCTUARY

Within this section of *From Disgrace to Grace*, you will find inspirational Bible scriptures, spiritual short poems, and uplifting spiritual sayings by various artists and websites. I'm dedicating a special section to my dear mother, a writer of spiritual poems; she inspired others with her talent. I hope that this section will bring inspiration to you to live a better life. Place these affirmations within your heart, use them to enhance your spirituality, and study them to make them a part of your everyday life. Let them be uplifting to you and others to know the love of God.

A SPECIAL DEDICATION
TO MY MOTHER

I wish to recognize my dear and beloved mother, Mrs. Ethel T. Williams, who is no longer with us; may she rest in God's peace. She wrote inspirational, spiritual poems and sayings. She received the Golden Poet Award, and one of her pieces was to be inducted into the prestigious Homer Honor Society of International Poets. Here are some samples of her work. I am honored to include her poems in my book.

God Made Man to Rule the Land

In the beginning, God made the heavens and the land. After it was finished, he made man. Then to keep man from getting lonesome, he took from man's rib and made a companion called woman, and they were as happy as a couple could be till Satan tempted woman to eat from the forbidden tree!

Then woman said to man, "You're blind and can't see. If you want to be wise, take a bite with me." Man opened his eyes to what he thought was grand, but what he saw was *woe unto man*! He'd been tempted by woman to disobey God's command.

Poor man went to work by the sweat of his brow. Woman bore children and kept the house. Man worked hard every day, and woman stayed home and demanded his pay. Yet man couldn't please woman, no matter how hard he tried; with all he did, she was never satisfied.

So man began to complain to woman one day: "I'm getting tired of your demands and the bossy things you say." Woman became bossier; she fretted and nagged every day. Man decided it was easier to let her have her way.

The beauty of an old man is the white hair on his head, but if he heeds a woman, he'll be bald instead. The strength of a young man lies in his hair, but when Delilah deceived Samson, he had strength nowhere.

The head of a man is Christ; the head of a woman is man. How man let woman get ahead of him, I cannot understand! God made man to rule over the land and everything therein, and if man lets woman rule over him, I believe it's sin.

So stand up, men! Be a man! God made you ruler over the land. If woman heeds not your demands, you'll never rule in this land. So men, fear God and keep his demands, for this is the whole duty of man.

Ethel T. Williams

A Working Mother's Prayer

Oh Lord, I'm a working mother, and my heart is full and troubled as I kneel down to thee in prayer. Lord, take my children in your care, watch over them each night and day, and guide their feet—don't let them stray.

Sometimes I must leave them alone to prepare a better home, but if I leave them in your hands, thy love will make them understand, for it will protect them from danger, confusion, hostility, drug addiction, and anger.

Lord, I know there's nothing you can't do if asked with faith and trust. Although sometimes they refuse to hear, don't leave them, Lord; just linger near. I know that as long as you are around, you will help them to bear their ups and downs.

As I kneel down before thee to pray, please guide my children, Lord, and show them the way!

Ethel T. Williams

A Mother's Love

A mother's love can't be measured, for it will never come to an end,

but it truly can be treasured! For she is your best friend!

She's with you when you're happy and with you when you're sad,

even when you are irritable or snappy and your attitude is bad!

And when you are sick and in trouble and others turn their back
   on you,

Mother is there on the double, doing all she can do.

And when you are lost and in despair and can't find peace anywhere,

remember your mother's prayers for you, asking God for blessings

that will see you safely through; she will be with you until the end,

for your mother is truly your best friend!

Ethel T. Williams

Welcoming You to Jesus

Welcoming you to Jesus, opening up your heart, getting to know him is a new start.

Just know you're always welcome to leave your problems outside the door,

to be filled with the Holy Spirit, and to sin no more!

Believe he died to save you, ask anything in his name,

and have faith without wavering, for you will never be the same.

We will be singing hallelujah and praising his holy name,

accepting his love without any shame. He has opened up his heart

to welcome you into his kingdom with a new start,

a true and sincere welcome from the bottom of his heart!

Ethel T. Williams

If God Went on Strike

If God should ever go on strike, it will be for the things he didn't like.

If he should ever give up and say, "That's it; no one wants to follow my way.

I've had enough of you, down on earth, disobeying my rules and going astray.

So this is what I'm going to do: I'll give my orders to condemn you.

Giving orders to the sun to cut off your heat supply and to run all the oceans dry,

telling the moon to give no more light so that you can't see throughout the night.

Then I'll make it really rough on you, by turning off your air supply too,

until every breath is gone, leaving no one to be known."

And he would be justified if fairness was the game,

for no one seems to obey or honor his name.

No one has been abused and treated with such disdain

as the name of Jesus, who loves us just the same.

He died to save us from our sins,

promising they will never be seen again.

He constantly has been tried by our deceit and all our lies.

When man says he wants a better deal, on strike he goes,

but what a deal we've given God, whom to everything we owe,

asking nothing of us but to believe in him, having faith and trust.

We don't care who we hurt or harm to get the things we like,

but what a mess we will all be in if God should go on strike!

Ethel T. Williams

Help Yourself to Jesus

Everyone, everywhere, seeks happiness, it's true,

but finding it and keeping it seems difficult to do.

Difficult because we think that happiness is found

only in places where wealth and fame abound.

So we go on searching in places of pleasure, seeking

recognition and monetary treasure, unaware that

happiness is just a state of mind. It's in the reach

of everyone who takes time to be kind. By making

others happy, we will be happy too.

For happiness you give away returns to shine on you.

Ethel T. Williams

He Asks So Little and Gives So Much

What must I do
  to ensure peace of mind
  is the answer I'm seeking too hard to find?
How can I know
  what God wants me to be?
How can I tell
  what's expected of me?
Where can I go
  for guidance and aid to help me correct the errors I've made?
The answers are found in doing three things:
  Do justice
  Love kindness
  Walk humbly with God
Take these things as your rule and rod,
Knowing with God, nothing is hard.

Ethel T. Williams

SPIRITUAL POEMS BY THE AUTHOR

Expression of Love

Love is something everyone looks for but rarely finds.

They say love is sweet and love is blind.

God's love can't be found in the likes of mankind,

and while we are looking far and wide, the love we seek is deep inside.

It's always present in our spirit, but we must learn to always share it.

Mary L. Robinson

Put Your Trust in God

Put your trust in God, for he will see you through

any circumstances that burden you.

For he is a person that does not lie.

He sent his son, Jesus Christ, to die,

to save you from all your sins, never to be seen again.

So trust in God with all your heart, changing your ways to do
  your part,

showing faith in all you do, knowing that he loves you.

And when that day of passing comes,

you will know you're his chosen one.

Mary L. Robinson

Faith

Faith is the key to kingdom living;

we must learn to love by giving.

Helping others, lifting up our brothers,

these are the things that please God,

touching deep within his heart.

Faith is all we need to get what God promised us.

We only get it by showing trust,

putting all our faith in him,

obeying his laws, and doing his will.

Our faith has to impact the way we live,

for the laws about disobedience are definitely real.

When you make the choice to decide,

just know with God, you can't lose.

You have to obey and do his commands.

Faith will get you to the promised land.

Mary L. Robinson

In the Presence of God

The presence of God surrounds you with a hedge of protection,
leading you in the right direction.
He says he will never leave or forsake you;
what he says is very true:
"Just come to me, and I'll give you rest."
Giving you a brand-new start to accept me into your heart,
showering you with unconditional love
that you can only get from above.
While you're walking in his light,
he will guard you day and night.
The love he gives is like no other;
it's the love we should have for each other.
In the presence of God, we should have no fear,
knowing that he is always near.
Our God is an awesome God, and his mercy endures forever.
In his presence we're safe and sound,
knowing he will always be around.
He saved us from evils that lurk within
when he rescued us from sin.
For in the presence of God,
believe he's got your back, and you've got his heart!

Mary L. Robinson

Judgment Day

Judgment day will surely come,
where God will judge everyone;
not all will make it, only some.
Your name must be in the Book of Life,
for it will prove you lived right,
obeying all of God's commands,
refusing to give into Satan's demands.
He is full of lies and deceit,
destroying the flesh, for he knows it's weak.
God is the one you should seek;
he's the one to keep you on your feet.
God only wants to show he cares;
it's your life he wants to spare.
Let's hope it's not too late
to walk through the pearly gates.
When that day of judgment comes,
you want to be among the blessed ones
with God saying, "Well done!"

Mary L. Robinson

SELECTED BIBLE VERSES

Although some of these Bible quotations appear earlier in the book, I've collected a list of verses I find particularly encouraging and inspiring.

"If God is for us, who can ever be against us" (Rom 8:31, NLT).

"For he shall give his angels charge over thee, to keep thee in all thy ways" (Ps 91:11, KJV).

"'For I know the plans I have for you,' says the Lord. 'They are plans for good and not for disaster, to give you a future and a hope'" (Jer 29:11, NLT).

"That your faith should not stand in the wisdom of men, but in the power of God" (1 Cor 2:5, KJV).

"Wisdom is the principle thing; therefore get wisdom: and with all thy getting get understanding" (Prv 4:7, KJV).

"I tell you the truth, unless you turn from your sins and become like little children, you will never get into the Kingdom of Heaven" (Mt 18:3, NLT).

"With their words, the godless destroy their friends, but knowledge will rescue the righteous" (Prv 11:9, NLT).

"Give honor to marriage, and remain faithful to one another in marriage. God will surely judge people who are immoral and those that commit adultery" (Heb 13:4, NLT).

"Come to me, all of you who are weary and carry heavy burdens, and I will give you rest" (Mt 11:28, NLT).

"Love never gives up, never loses faith, is always hopeful, and endures through every circumstance" (1 Cor 13:7, NLT).

"The thief cometh not, but for to steal, and to kill, and to destroy: I am come that they might have life, and that they might have it more abundantly" (Jn 10:10, KJV).

"For God so loved the world, that he gave his only begotten Son, that whosoever believeth in him should not perish, but have everlasting life" (Jn 3:16, KJV).

"I can do all things through Christ which strengtheneth me" (Phil 4:13, KJV).

SPIRITUAL SAYINGS
Taken from Godly Woman Daily

Dear God, no matter what happens, give me a heart that's willing to obey.

God has a wonderful way of turning negatives into positives.

Don't let anyone tell you, you can't do something when the Bible says you can do all things through Christ.

Look forward and trust God.

Look around and serve God.

Look up and find God.

Look back and thank God.

Pray, relax, let go, and let God take over.

Only God can turn a mess into a message,

A test into a trial,

A trial into a triumph,

A victim into victory.

God is good at all times.

Life isn't about finding yourself; it's about discovering who you are.

When you pray for others, God listens to you and blesses them, and sometimes, when you are safe and happy, remember that someone prayed for you:

Every second

Every minute

Every hour

Every day.

God is with you.

GOD'S COMMANDMENTS

I'm ending this book with the Ten Commandments. I have observed that a lot of people don't know all of them. Even I was guilty of this. We need to acknowledge the Ten Commandments; they're our key to eternal life.

These commandments are under the old covenant, which was created for the nonbelievers to show them how sinful they were. However, these laws don't apply to the born-again Christians, for they are under the new covenant, which is God's grace, where their faith enables them to overcome all sin. They are led by the spirit, not the law. In scripture (Gal 2:16), it says that a person is made right with God by faith in Jesus Christ, not by obeying the law. When you are a believer, your spirit leads you to live a godly life, for you are the righteousness of God and the law does not apply to you in that manner.

Satan has a lot to do with our tendencies to break God's laws. He supplies us with counterfeit laws that are deceitful and that destroy our lives. He uses sins such as adultery, fornication, sexual immorality, and divorce as weapons against us when we disobey.

When we allow sinful behaviors in our life, we send the message that we believe it's the right way to live. Instead, we have to use our discernment to choose between right and wrong, for God has supplied us with wisdom to know better than what the world considers acceptable.

So when making your choice, choose to become a believer, giving your life to God by having faith and trust in him, so that you can live under his grace, for no man is capable of keeping these laws in his own strength. You need Jesus Christ, your savior.)

THE TEN COMMANDMENTS

Thou shalt have no other gods before me.

Thou shalt not make unto thee any graven image.

Thou shalt not take the name of the Lord thy God in vain.

Remember the Sabbath day, to keep it holy.

Honor thy father and thy mother.

Thou shalt not kill.

Thou shalt not commit adultery.

Thou shalt not steal.

Thou shalt not bear false witness against thy neighbor.

Thou shalt not covet anything that is thy neighbor's.

Take these commandments, which were created to show non-believers their sins, put them in your hearts, making them part of your lifestyle. However, once you become a born-again Christian, you're no longer under these commandments, you are under God's grace, which enables you not to sin. God gave you the gift of free will, so you get to determine whether you choose to obey God, or keep doing it Satan's way.

REFERENCES

Biblical quotations are taken from the King James Version (KJV), the New Living Translation (NLT), or the New International Version (NIV), as indicated in each instance.

Cathedral wall engraving. In *How to Find God: Living Water for Those Who Thirst*. Carol Stream, IL: Tyndale House Publishers, 2004.

Dollar, Creflo. *Changing Your World*. TBN. Television broadcast.

Fernandez, Henry. Message at weekly Sunday morning service. The Faith Center, Lauderhill, FL.

Godly Woman Daily. www.godlywoman.co.

Hagee, John P. *John Hagee Today*. TBN. Television broadcast.

Osteen, Joel. *Joel Osteen*. GEB. Television broadcast.

Robinson, Mary L. Selected poems. In the author's possession. August 2012.

Williams, Ethel T. Selected poems. In the author's possession.